CHAMPIONSHIP GAMES

I0878818

SOCCER'S WORLD CUP

PERCY LEED

LERNER PUBLICATIONS ◆ MINNEAPOLIS

Copyright © 2025 by Lerner Publishing Group, Inc.

All rights reserved. International copyright secured. No part of this book may be reproduced, stored in a retrieval system, or transmitted in any form or by any means—electronic, mechanical, photocopying, recording, or otherwise—without the prior written permission of Lerner Publishing Group, Inc., except for the inclusion of brief quotations in an acknowledged review.

Lerner Publications Company
An imprint of Lerner Publishing Group, Inc.
241 First Avenue North
Minneapolis, MN 55401 USA

For reading levels and more information, look up this title at www.lernerbooks.com.

Main body text set in Mikado.
Typeface provided by HVD Fonts.

Photo Editor: Nicole Berglund

Library of Congress Cataloging-in-Publication Data

Names: Leed, Percy, 1968- author.
Title: Soccer's World Cup / Percy Leed.
Description: Minneapolis, MN : Lerner Publications, [2025] | Series: Lerner sports rookie. Championship games | Includes bibliographical references and index. | Audience: Ages 5–8 | Audience: Grades K–1 | Summary: "Soccer is the planet's most popular sport, and the Men's World Cup and Women's World Cup are its biggest events. Meet the players, relive the games, and get a behind-the-scenes look at soccer's greatest showcase"— Provided by publisher.
Identifiers: LCCN 2024013107 (print) | LCCN 2024013108 (ebook) | ISBN 9798765648049 (library binding) | ISBN 9798765661529 (paperback) | ISBN 9798765653951 (epub)
Subjects: LCSH: World Cup (Soccer)—Juvenile literature.
Classification: LCC GV943.49 .L44 2025 (print) | LCC GV943.49 (ebook) | DDC 796.334/66809—dc23/eng/20240328

LC record available at https://lccn.loc.gov/2024013107
LC ebook record available at https://lccn.loc.gov/2024013108

Manufactured in the United States of America
1-1010913-53365-6/27/2024

TABLE OF CONTENTS

CHAPTER 1
THE WORLD CUP

Spain and England played in the 2023 Women's World Cup. The winner would be the world champion.

A Spain player kicked the ball.

Goal! Spain won the game 1–0.

The 1930 US Men's World Cup team

World Cups take place every four years. The first Men's World Cup was in 1930. Uruguay won it.

The Women's World Cup began in 1991. The United States was the first champion.

CHAPTER 2 GREATEST MOMENTS

In 1986, superstar Diego Maradona had the ball. He ran past many players to score for Argentina.

Cameroon played Argentina at the next Men's World Cup. Cameroon lost two players during the game. But they still won!

The US and China played in the 1999 Women's World Cup. The teams were tied when US player Brandi Chastain scored. Team USA won!

Hakan Şükür scored for Turkey in 2002. The goal came less than 11 seconds into the game. It was the fastest goal in World Cup history.

CHAPTER 3
BEST PLAYERS

Pelé played in four Men's World Cups for Brazil.

He scored 12 goals for his team.

Diego Maradona was the best player at the 1986 Men's World Cup. He led Argentina to the title.

Abby Wambach scored 14 Women's World Cup goals. She helped the US win in 2015.

Marta scored 17 goals for Brazil at six Women's World Cups. No one has ever scored more.

Megan Rapinoe scored six goals at the 2019 Women's World Cup. She helped Team USA win the title.

Many fans think Lionel Messi is the world's best player. He helped Argentina win the 2022 Men's World Cup.

CHAPTER 4 WORLD CUP FUN

The World Cups move around the world. Every four years, they take place in a different country.

Billions of people watch the World Cups on TV.

Fans pack World Cup stadiums. They wear their country's colors and cheer for the team. The World Cup is fun for all!

FIFA WOMEN'S
ORLD CUP 2023

WORLD CUP CHAMPS

Here are recent World Cup winners:

Women's World Cup

- **2023** Spain
- **2019** United States
- **2015** United States
- **2011** Japan
- **2007** Germany

Men's World Cup

- **2022** Argentina
- **2018** France
- **2014** Germany
- **2010** Spain
- **2006** Italy

FUN FACTS

Brazil has won the most Men's World Cup titles. They have won five times.

The United States is the leader in Women's World Cup titles. They have won four World Cups.

In 2023, almost two million fans watched Women's World Cup games in person.

GLOSSARY

stadium: a large building where public events take place

superstar: a great player

title: a championship

LEARN MORE

Chaffee, Kim. *Courage in Her Cleats: The Story of Soccer Star Abby Wambach*. Salem, MA: Page Street Kids, 2023.

Leed, Percy. *Soccer: A First Look*. Minneapolis: Lerner Publications, 2023.

Rose, Rachel. *Megan Rapinoe: Soccer Superstar*. Minneapolis: Bearport, 2021.

INDEX

PHOTO ACKNOWLEDGMENTS

Image credits: AP Photo/Kim Price/Cal Sport Media, p. 4; History and Art Collection/Alamy, p. 6; TOMMY CHENG/Getty Images, p. 7; Bongarts/Getty Images, p. 8; PCN Photography/Alamy, p. 10; Onze/Getty Images, p. 11; Action Plus Sports Images/Alamy, p. 12; AP Photo/picture-alliance/dpa, p. 13; dpa picture alliance archive/Alamy, p. 14; Jonathan Larsen/Diadem Images/Alamy, p. 15; Aflo Co. Ltd./Alamy, p. 16; Powerpics/Alamy, p. 17; AP Photo/Abbie Parr, p. 18; AP Photo/Dmitri Lovetsky, p. 19; AP Photo/Daniela Porcelli/SPP/Sipa USA, p. 21. Design elements: Winner Creative/Shutterstock. Cover: AP Photo/Kim Price/Cal Sport Media.